The Little
Warhoı

Catherine de Duve
In co-operation with BAM (Beaux-Arts Mons)

Discover the life and work of the star of Pop Art

BEAUX-ARTS MONS

KATE'ART
EDITIONS

AT THE TIME OF

In the 50s and 60s, the economy of the United States is booming. New cars such as the Cadillac and Mustang, new appliances such as the vacuum cleaner and washing machine, as well as other new manufactured objects help make it a consumer society.

It's a "consumer society".

You drink *Coca-Cola*, *Campbell's* soup and strawberry milkshakes. You eat Kellogg's cornflakes, popcorn and ketchup. You use *Brillo* soap! Posters, advertising and the cinema make you dream… Do they show the path to happiness or an unrealistic dream? Even Hollywood stars are products of this mass consumer society. Everything must shine!

The jukeboxes play "the King", Elvis Presley, the idol of the younger generation. You dance in night clubs to a whole mix of ballads, salsa, cha-cha and rock 'n' roll. To earn money quickly is the dream. Everyone can try!

The television starts to appear in the home. Neil Armstrong walks on the moon! You read magazines and American "comics". Do you know them? Superman, Mickey Mouse, Captain America…

This is the "American Dream"! However, the Vietnam War and the threat of nuclear weapons in Cuba dampen enthusiasm.

POP ART

In the 60s, called the "Golden Sixties", society is changing through more freedom and equality. Women wear mini-skirts and bikinis! You dance to the sound of the Beatles. The Hippie movement is changing the world! "Peace and love"!

At this time abstract expressionist art is in vogue. Colours and shapes are painted without reference to objects or people. Art evolves! Artists, first in Britain and then in the United States, create a new artistic movement inspired by pop culture images from newspapers and magazines, daily objects and people... It's **Pop Art**!

Warhol becomes the leader of the movement, "the Pope of the Pop".

Who are the other American artists of Pop Art? What do they paint? Jaspers John paints the American flag, Robert Rauschenberg reuses images from the media, Roy Lichtenstein mimics the style of comics. But what is Andy Warhol going to create?

Warhol paints a portrait of Rauschenberg in 1967

3

ANDY WARHOL

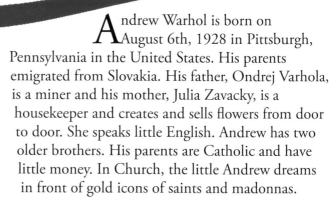

Andrew Warhol is born on August 6th, 1928 in Pittsburgh, Pennsylvania in the United States. His parents emigrated from Slovakia. His father, Ondrej Varhola, is a miner and his mother, Julia Zavacky, is a housekeeper and creates and sells flowers from door to door. She speaks little English. Andrew has two older brothers. His parents are Catholic and have little money. In Church, the little Andrew dreams in front of gold icons of saints and madonnas.

At 9 years old, Andrew falls ill and often has to stay with his mum. He likes to flip through magazines, read comics and draw as he listens to the radio. He often goes to the movies and collects pictures of celebrities. One day he receives a camera. It is a revelation! At home he watches cartoons. Introverted, he creates his universe full of celebrities.

Aged 14, Andrew loses his father. After school he begins studying art at the Carnegie Institute of Technology. He decorates the windows of a department store. The son of poor immigrants, America fascinates him. Andrew dreams of becoming rich and famous.

 What is Superman saying? Complete the bubble.

A ged 21, Andrew moves to New York and calls himself "Andy Warhol". He works as an illustrator. In 1949, Glamour asks him for drawings of women's shoes. Warhol is inspired. There is already talk of him as "the best shoe artist in New York"!

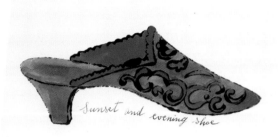

Sunset and evening shoe

But the young advertiser wants to become an artist! An artist like no other…
In 1952 he holds his first exhibition. His mother joins him in New York. They live in a small apartment. Warhol, curious, wants to explore its culture. He often goes to the cinema and the opera, attends dance performances, collects art and tours the world with a friend for seven weeks.

 It's your turn! Design the cover of a major magazine. Imagine a beautiful shoe!

VOGUE

BAZAAR
Harper's

AT THE DINNER TABLE

Warhol brings the everyday into art. Like all Americans, he remembers eating *Campbell's* soup in his childhood. In 1961 the artist chooses "the" can of soup and paints it "coldly". It looks like it's real!

With the help of stencils, he reproduces the lettering and decorative style in a larger size. That's how Warhol keeps the ordinary in a work of art!

In 1962, Andy Warhol exhibits his cans in Los Angeles. Lined up like in the store, the lovers of soup… and art, are shocked. "Come on! Make an art gallery in a supermarket?" Warhol attracts attention. He reaches his goal. The artist adds a ladle and makes a series of 32 varieties of soup: Beef Consommé, Tomato- Beef Noodle, Black Beans… What flavour do you prefer?

Look at these two cans of soup. They look real! Which would you taste?

Design the label of your favourite soup.

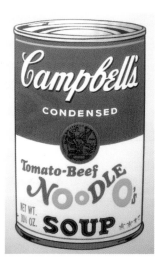

COCA-COLA

Pop and pop culture! Warhol chooses images that everyone can recognise at a glance: celebrities, soup, shower curtains, coca-cola bottles… He draws all these modern things as they appear. In the United States the brands of *Campbell's* soup, *Coca-Cola* and *Heinz* ketchup are consumed by all. Everywhere people have the same taste. Pop Art is for everyone!

> *What is extraordinary about America is that it is the first country to have established the custom that the richest consumers buy the same things as the poorest. You watch TV while drinking Coca-Cola, and you know that the President drinks Coke, Liz Taylor drinks it, and you think, you can drink Coke too. Coke is Coke, and no wealth in the world can get you a better Coke.*

What do you think of this quote from Andy Warhol? Is this still the case today?

For his first model of a Coke bottle, Warhol took out an advert in the newspaper *Byzantine Catholic World* from his mother. He will soon reproduce it in a series of industrial bottles. Warhol loves art in industrial quantities!

How many bottles of Coke can you count?

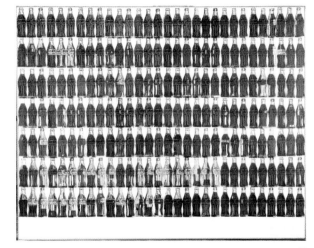

SCREEN-PRINT

In 1962 Andy Warhol begins to use a printing technique usually reserved for graphic screen printing. This process can produce works of art in a **series**. From a single image you can make many variations.

Here is a portrait of the Belgian painter Paul Delvaux. Do you know him?

Look at the different variations. In your opinion what colour contrasts and shapes work well in this portrait? How are the strokes applied and with what tool? A brush, a paint roller, a sponge or scissors?

TECHNIQUE

The materials

- **A screen**: this consists of a canvas on a frame. The canvas is polyester pierced with small holes.
- **A film**: a transparent film on which the printed image is reproduced. What is black will be in colour, and the transparent parts will become the outline of the stencil.
- **A UV lamp**
- **A scraper**
- **Ink**

The screen-printing technique

- Completely cover the screen of the photosensitive film, which reacts with the light. Then allow the sheet to dry in the dark for at least 24 hours.

- The film is placed under the frame. The film and frame are exposed to light through a UV lamp. UV light cooks the material. The material hardens, except where the image is black. Where it is black the small holes remain open so that the ink can flow. The fabric is then rinsed.

- The canvas becomes the stencil and is set on a table. Using the scraper, the image is printed on the material underneath (t-shirt, paper, canvas…). The printing is done in two steps: 1) Topping: Gently deposit the ink on the stencil 2) Printing: The ink is spread by passing it through the small holes in the stencil.

Each colour corresponds to a stencil in a different way.
And there you have it! A print!

Warhol also likes this method because it leaves it to chance. You never know in advance and cannot predict the final outcome. Even if they are multiplied, each painting is different and remains unique. The artist adds touches of colour with a brush. Warhol only needs to sign them!

MARILYN

In August 1962, the great Hollywood star Marilyn Monroe committed suicide. Warhol immortalises this tragic event. The artist is fascinated by the beauty and enduring popularity of the actress.

What is Warhol's secret? He cuts out advertising photographs of Marilyn taken from the 1953 film *Niagara*. It is then photographed and made into a stencil that he uses for the entire production of the series of portraits. The artist multiplies Marilyn. Only the size and colours vary: pink, yellow, black and gold.

Marilyn shines like a Madonna. This is the most dazzling Warhol icon. It represents the glamorous, successful, but also tragic side to Marilyn.

Here's the screen-printed Marilyn. What features are highlighted? Which do you prefer?

ICONS

Elvis Presley, Michael Jackson & Liz Taylor… these are the stars that inspire Warhol. They dream! Thanks to Andy they become a true "product of consumerism" together. They can be bought by everyone and so can decorate walls everywhere. You are left with the impression that they are part of your everyday lives, like ketchup, tomato soup and coca-cola. We call them by their first names: Marilyn, Elvis, Michael… And Warhol is "Andy Candy" of the stars!

The artist loves "cosmetic" beauty. You can see he uses make-up in his portraits. He retouches them.

What does he highlight? Like Warhol, colour the background with Pop colours!

JACKIE

Who is this distinguished lady? Is she famous? What does she do for a living? Is she a singer, actress, presenter or politician? It's Jacqueline Kennedy, "Jackie"! She is the wife of U.S. President John F. Kennedy who was assassinated on November 22nd 1963 in Dallas.

Here Jackie looks happy. Yet her life is turned upside down when her husband is assassinated at her side. The images of the drama replay on loop on television. The pain of the first lady of the United States is public and live. It belongs to all Americans.

Warhol creates several portraits of Jackie, sometimes smiling, sometimes crying at the funeral of her husband. It shows the fragile nature of happiness. Warhol says that every man will die one day.

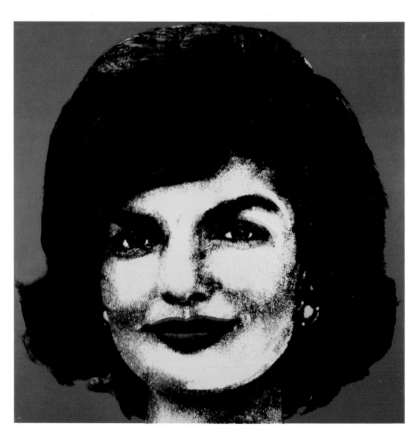

In Warhol's style, decorate the face of the elegant Jackie Kennedy. Apply her make-up and colour the background with a bright colour to highlight the portrait. Create a strong image that can be used to advertise or share a political message.

THE FACTORY

I want to be a machine to produce art!

Andy Warhol wants to produce paintings in series, in large quantities like a machine production! The technique of screen-printing helps this.

In 1964, Andy opens the "Factory" in a loft in the heart of Manhattan, New York. The artist works with many assistants, painters, actors, musicians and students. It is a true little art factory!

At night, the factory turns into a nightclub, hosting trendy "underground" parties, gathering the jet set and artists. The door is open to all! "They do not come to me" says Warhol "but to meet and see who comes." Everyone is curious and loves to share new experiences. Ideas will flourish. At the Factory everyone is considered a superstar. Andy loves to live in the midst of his "boys and girls".

Here is the "Silver Factory". Everything is painted silver. Warhol is surrounded by portraits. Do you recognise them?

POP MUSIC

What an atmosphere! The Factory is a meeting place for creativity. It has film screenings, exhibitions and concerts. Warhol is involved with everything. He produces films and collaborates with fellow artists like himself such as The Velvet Underground and Mick Jagger from the Rolling Stones. Andy designs the cover of The Velvet Underground's famous album.

Mick Jagger in 1975

It's your turn. Design the cover of an album by your favourite band.

FLOWERS

A ndy Warhol creates a series on the theme of flowers, "Flowers". The artist does not draw flowers but selects a photograph of hibiscus published in the magazine *Modern* Photography. Warhol asks his assistants to make the print.

In 1964, Warhol exhibits "Flowers" in New York. The walls of the Leo Castelli Gallery are covered in his work. It looks like floral wallpaper!

The next year, the same series is shown in Paris. More than a hundred paintings fill the Ileana Sonnabend Gallery. Andy goes to the launch. He loves shopping in Paris!

Look at these flowers. They seem like they are floating. The colours are artificial. Imagine a room full of flowers. What an effect! Would you like this wallpaper in your room?

FLOWER POWER

What is hidden in Warhol's flowers? Behind their decorative appearance the artist represents the transience of life. Everything is doomed to disappear one day.

Colour a "Flowers" series. Give the best possible colour to the flowers as they fade quickly. "We must take advantage of the beauty of life."

MAO

In February 1972, U.S. President Richard Nixon visits the Chinese head of state, Mao Zedong. This is a real event! It is a historic meeting for the two nations. The U.S. media reveal the face of the Chinese leader. Who is he?

In China, Mao is everywhere! The state organises propaganda and creates a cult around his image. He is considered a living god. His portrait is a popular icon. The American artist transforms the famous image of Mao into art! What interests Warhol is to work with images that are already incredibly famous.

 Look at how Warhol reinterprets the official portrait of the Chinese leader.

WALLPAPER

Wallpaper Pattern

Who is Mao? Mao Zedong is a founding member of the Chinese Communist Party. In 1949 he proclaims the People's Republic of China. He organises the Great Cultural Revolution. Through this he closes many schools and executes thousands of intellectuals. It forces millions of Chinese into manual labour. His Little Red Book offers summaries of his speeches. At the time it is the second most read book after the Bible.

In 1974, Warhol exhibits his portraits of Mao at the Galliera Museum in Paris. These are hung on a wallpaper designed with the image of Mao. After the colourful flowers and cow-heads, Mao equally becomes a decorative pattern.

It's your go! Create a new version of this wallpaper using the portrait of Mao.

STAR-ARTIST

Warhol becomes a star himself. Andy also produces numerous self-portraits and becomes an American myth in his own right!

Who is hiding behind this camouflage? Warhol creates a mysterious **self-portrait**. Do you see him? Ill at ease, Warhol carefully crafts a public image. He wants to both hide and show himself. His personal identity disappears behind this public image. He hides behind this camouflage, disguised in white and wearing a wig!

Warhol uses the technique of superimposing: one image on another. Neon pink for the face, camouflage to hide, then the artist is surrounded by black paint. It shines!

What a look! What a hairstyle! Is Warhol a punk? What do you think of these colours?

WIG

Warhol goes bald aged 21. He wears wigs. He collects them : blonde, gray, silver, or multi-toned. "Be somebody with a body", that is to say, become someone with presence. Andy creates his own unique and instantly recognisable style.

Andy often visits his favourite wigmaker who runs an elegant shop near the Factory. The artist tries both male and female wigs. He has over a hundred in his collection.

Disguise yourself like Warhol! Draw yourself in a wig. Put sunglasses on and try to camouflage yourself.

SHOWBIZ

*I started in commercial art and I want
to finish with a company based around art…
Being good in business is the most fascinating art form…
Making money is art and working is art.
Good business is the greatest form of art.*

For Warhol, to work is an art form, and to earn money is another.
He wants to become a real "artist-businessman". He is a true entrepreneur.
He produces music, movies, videos, opens a nightclub, writes books,
edits magazines (*Interview*), and has his own TV show. Showbiz!

"Are you successful?" The dollar
is also at the heart of American
society, the emblem of real
success. In the 60s, the American
artist draws dollars in a series of
paintings. He finds that the dollar
bills are "well designed" and
redraws them tirelessly.

How would you earn your first dollar? Imagine a new type
of money. What colour would you choose? Draw it below.

22

DOLLAR

Warhol often repeats the same themes throughout his career: coke bottles, Campbell's soup, Marilyn, dollars, etc...

In 1981, the artist reduces the dollar bill to its simplest expression, the "$" symbol. Art and money come together.

Warhol has a sense of humour. He believes that instead of buying a valuable painting, it is better to hang paintings of the dollar sign on the wall. Visitors will see the money directly on the wall and therefore see its value. How ironic!

Imagine a new piece around the sign of your choice: £, €, $.

PORTRAITS

In the 70 and 80s, celebrities, movie stars, artists, bankers and businessmen are scrambling to get their portrait done by Warhol. It is a must! Warhol did not lose his business sense. If you pay $25,000 a signed Warhol portrait is yours!

 Who am I? Find the great fashion designer Giorgio Armani. What style would you choose for your portrait? Which looks like diamond dust?

TRICK

"Everyone is beautiful!"

To get a good Polaroid portrait, Warhol makes his model pose for many hours. He glosses over the models in white to bring out their facial features. The goal is to make a beautiful portrait! A sublime image. The artist also wants to make portraits of his young artist friends such as Keith Haring & Basquiat.

MY EXHIBITION

In 1983, a Swiss art dealer offers to organise an exhibition of his drawings of children's toys. He creates a series of prints from images of "vintage" mechanical toys he has collected for years.

Finally, an exhibition for kids!

Specially designed for them, children come to the show and discover the work of Warhol. You can discover printed versions of old toys: cosmonauts, monkeys, parrots, dogs, fish, clowns, pandas, planes, boats, robots, trains and much more…

It's your turn. Create your own exhibition.
Draw your favourite toys.

ELECTRIC CHAIR

> *You cannot imagine the number of people who would hang a picture of an electric chair in their living room, especially if the colours go well with the curtains.*

Here is an electric chair, a symbol of death. What a strange subject for a painting! Who has been sentence to death? There is no one, just a chair in the middle of an empty room. "Is anyone there?" Death lurks… What a strange feeling of absence and emptiness.
This painting represents the other side of the mirror, the dark side of America.
The artist trivializes everything! It is a torture machine, but a work of art.
He adds a "flashy" layer. Here is the yellow version, but do you prefer the pink? At the time, the use of the electric chair is part of a debate about capital punishment. What does Warhol think about it?

Look at the painting. Write your impression of the piece below.

I feel _____

KNIVES

I realised that everything I do is connected to death.

The theme of death fascinates Andy Warhol who fears it. The death of his father deeply affected him. Since the 60s the artist evokes death in his work.

Warhol throws nothing away. He collects photos, Polaroids, tickets, souvenirs and clippings. It is from his archives that he draws these shocking images: plane crashes, car accidents, the assassination of President Kennedy, the atomic bomb…

Later, the artist creates this "still life" of knives. Or is it a portrait of American society? These are impressive! Giant knives! The Painting measures 2.28 m x 1.77 m.

Look at these knives. What do you make of the painting? Are they weapons or kitchen utensils?

COWBOY

Do you recognise this man dressed as a cowboy drawing his pistol? Does he want to duel with you? It's Elvis Presley, the famous singer and actor! He performs in Westerns. Here he is in the movie *Flaming Star*, released in 1960. At the time Elvis was at the height of his success. A real idol! Warhol was fascinated by him and multiplies his image to infinity as a set of reflections in a mirror. What does he hide behind the mirror? In 1963, this series is shown at the Ferus Gallery in Los Angeles.

Have you ever watched a film from this period? Cowboys and gangsters always have guns. Elvis collects them.

Look at the multiple portrait. It is a full length portrait. What does the gun in Elvis' hand represent? Imagine what he's saying.

BANG BANG

In 1968, Warhol is 39 years old. He is the victim of an attempted assassination. An actress with whom he had worked with on one of his films, Valerie Solanas, shot him with a pistol at close range. He is believed dead, but he survives. Seriously injured, he spends two months in hospital. After this event Warhol becomes obsessed with his health and his own death. He wears corsets and exercises daily with his personal trainer.

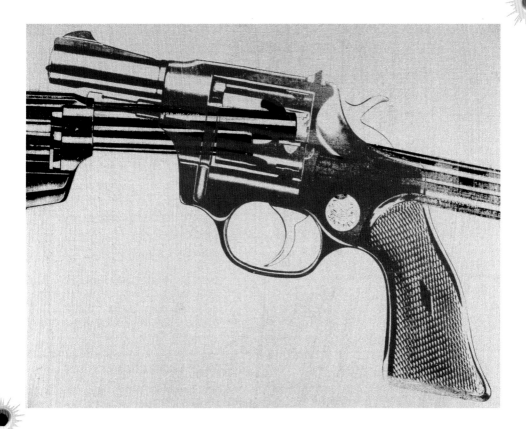

In the United States, the gun is a symbol strongly anchored in the collective imagination. A symbol of power, the gun is the pride of American culture.

JESUS SUPERSTAR

In the late 70s, Warhol is inspired by famous masterpieces of the Italian Renaissance, such as the *Mona Lisa* by da Vinci and Botticelli's *Venus*. The artist often depicts religious scenes. In 1986, Warhol reproduces a masterpiece!

The Last Supper by Leonardo da Vinci is a fresco painted in 1498. It is preserved in Milan, Italy. What does it represent? Jesus Christ called for his last meal with his twelve disciples, but Judas denounces Christ, who is then arrested and sentenced to death on the cross.

Warhol has a picture of *The Last Summer* offered by his mother that he treasures in his prayer book. The artist interprets this a hundred different ways, sometimes in whole, sometimes split, sometime only highlighting one detail.

Everything is pink. How many characters can you see? What are they eating? Find Jesus and Judas. Why has Warhol put these two identical images together?

Is life not just a series of images that change as they repeat themselves?

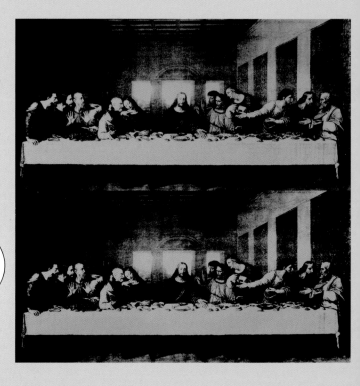

In secret, Andy Warhol is deeply religious and often takes refuge in the church under the candle light and prayers. This is privacy. He is afraid of the passing of time, death and disease. He consumes life without moderation. He collects photographs, and films with a 16 mm camera and a VCR recorder which he uses to explore life, people, society, the stars and the Empire State Building.

Just like his work, Warhol is a symbol. He is the American dream of success, glamour and daring. He opens the way to a new type of artist for the twentieth century.

Andy Warhol dies on the 22nd February 1987 in New York, aged 58, from complications due to surgery. The Warhol Museum later opens in 1994 in Pittsburgh, his hometown.

· T H E   E N D ·

Text: Catherine de Duve
Graphics: Véronique Lux and Kate'Art Editions
Design: Kate'Art Editions
Research: Julie Verschueren, Margaux De Jonckere and Camille Fraipont
Proofreading: Isabelle Gérard
Translation: Stuart Forward

Andy Warhol

LONDON: Saatchi collection: *Triple Elvis,* 1962 (silk screen on canvas): cover, p. 11, p. 28
PRIVATE COLLECTION: *Marilyn, right hand side,* 1964: cover (detail), p. 10, *Mick Jagger* (colour sprintscreen), 1975: p. 15 (detail), *Mao,* 1972: p. 18, *Mao,* 1972 (silk screen on paper): p. 19
KNOKKE: **Collection Gallery Adrian David**: *Robert Rauschenberg,* 1967 (silk screen on canvas): p. 3, *Butterfly,* 1958 (Ink and Aquarelle on paper): cover, p. 3, p. 31, *Self-portrait,* 1967 (Red enamel on white vinyl): p. 4, p. 27, *Campbell's Soup I (Consommé Beef),* 1968 (silk screen on paper): p. 6, *Campbell's Soup II (Tomato Beef Noodle),* 1969 (silk screen on paper): p. 6, *Paul Delvaux,* 1981 (Acrylic and silk screen on canvas): p. 8, *Committee 2000,* 1982 (Acrylic and silk screen on canvas): p. 14, *Flowers,* 1964 (Acrylic on canvas): p. 17, *Caroline Law,* 1975 (Acrylic on canvas): p. 24, *Mario Borsato,* 1981 (Acrylic on canvas): p. 24, *Armani,* 1981 (Acrylic on canvas and diamant dust): p. 24
PITTSBURG: Collection of The Andy Warhol Museum, Pittsburgh: Founding Collection, Contribution The Andy Warhol Foundation for the Visual Arts, Inc.
Self-portrait, 1986 (Acrylic and ink silk screen on canvas): p. 1, p. 20, *Marilyn (4),* c.1978 (Acrylic and silk screen on canvas): p. 10 (detail), *Red Jackie,* 1964 (Acrylic and ink silk screen on canvas): cover, p. 12, *Mao Wallpaper,* 1974: p. 19, *Dollar sign,* 1981 (Acrylic and ink silk screen on canvas): p. 23, *Little Electric Chair,* 1964-1965 (Acrylic and ink silk screen): p. 26, *Knives,* 1981-1982 (Acrylic and ink silk screen on canvas): p. 27, *Gun,* 1981-1982 (Acrylic and ink silk screen): p. 29
SONDRIO: Collection Credito Valtellinese, *The Last Supper,* 1986 (Acrylic and silk screen on canvas): p. 30
The Bridgeman Art Library: *Sunst and Evening Shor, from 'À la recherche du shoe perdu'* (hand-coloured letterpress), c.1955: p. 5 Photo ©Christie's Images/The Bridgeman Art, *210 Coca-Cola Bottles,* 1962: p. 7 Photo ©Christie's Images/The Bridgeman Art, *Flowers,* 1970 (Acrylic on canvas): p. 16 Photo ©Christie's Images/The Bridgeman Art, *Two Dollar Bill* (silk screen on canvas), 1962: p. 22 Photo ©Christie's Images/The Bridgeman Art, *Clockwork Panda Clockwork Panda* (synthetic polymer silkscreened on canvas), 1983: p. 25 Photo ©Christie's Images/The Bridgeman Art

Photographies:
Collection Dagli Orti/Mondadori Portfolio: *The American artist Andy Warhol sitting in his studio. Some paintings depict Jacqueline Kennedy,* New York, 1964: p. 14

Illustrations:
Classic Juke-box: p. 2 ©Pixel embargo-Fotolia: p. 2, *Coca-Cola*: cover, p. 2, *Campbell's Soup*: cover, p. 2, *Vector retro tv*: p. 2 ©FreeSoulProduction-Fotolia: p. 2, *Superhero*: p. 2, p. 4 ©Ianrward- Fotolia.com, *Statue of Liberty, USA*: p. 5 ©Etravler -Fotolia.com: p. 5, *Niagara*: p. 10, *Wig*: p. 21 ©Freischnauze- Fotolia.com

With thanks to: Xavier Roland, Manager of the Mons Museum Centre, Joëlle Kapompole, Deputy of Culture for Mons, Alice Cantigniau, Officer for Culture, Géraldine Simonet, Officer for Distribution, Véronique Lux, Julie Verschueren, Margaux De Jonckere, Camille Fraipont, Géraldine Dubois, «Les ateliers de sérigraphie Bikini» (www. atelierbikini.be) and all those who contributed to the creation of this book.

Our books are available in various languages: English, French, German, Dutch, Spanish, Italian, Russian, Japanese and Danish.

www.kateart.com